A SERIES OF JESUS' POWERFUL WORDS

Whoever keeps Jesus' word will never see death.

(John 8, 51)

Book III

The Parables Told by Jesus

Book I: **The Life of Jesus**

Book II: **The Teachings of Jesus
About the Trinity**

Book III: **The Parables Told by
Jesus**

Book IV: **The Teachings of Jesus**

Book V: **Jesus, the Miracle Maker**

THE PARABLES TOLD BY JESUS

The most glorious parables from the gospels of Matthew, Mark, Luke and John light up our path through this world and show us how to avoid the wrong way by preparing us for our final destination

Prepared by
Peter Naumovich, Ph.D.

Naum Publishing

Grand Island, New York

Address all Inquires to the Publisher:
Naum Publishing
124 Colonial Drive
Grand Island, NY 14072
(716) 240 -7856

Editor: Peter Naumovich, Ph.D.
Technical Editor: Borka Naumovich, M.S.

This volume is published and printed in 2016
Copyright © 2016 by Naum Publishing
NPV32

Front cover: Icon of The Mother of God, by priest Kiprian,
1958, St. Stephen Serbian Orthodox Church, Lackawan-
na, New York. Photo Naum Publishing with permission.
The Illustrations: a) "The Bible Gallery, Illustrated by
Gustave Dore"- by Talbot Chambers, New York, 1880;
b) "The Bible Illustrations" by Gustave Dore, Moscow
2002

Library of Congress Control Number: 2016910317

ISBN 978-0-9830926-2-9

Printed in the United States of America

PREFACE

Our Lord, Jesus Christ, once said: " ... *the word that you hear is not mine, but the Father's who sent me.*" (John 14, 24)

This Bible verse illustrates our only guideline: to compile all the words, thoughts and parables and extract and collect them so that they could be available and useful. All five books contain only verses of the New Testament, because it was only possible way to find these valuable and necessary thoughts and lessons.

Our Lord, Jesus Christ, by executing a task that the Father gave him left us as the most precious treasure of all: the Father's words and thoughts to help us in trouble, until his coming again.

To obtain a true picture of our Savior, his accomplishments and his triumphant resurrection, sometimes it is necessary, apart from the words of Jesus, to cite the thought and words of St. John the Baptist or the apostles. These men were eye-witnesses of the events, all the humiliation and all suffering to which our Savior was exposed, all his short life.

These books consist of the words, thoughts, sayings and parables of our Lord Himself and they are accepted in all Christian churches.

Archaic Words

art = are

lo = look, see

thee = You
thine = Yours
thou = You
thy = Your

thou didst send = You sent
thou gavest = You have given
thou hast given = You have given
thou hast sent = You have sent
thou hast loved = You have loved
thou shouldst take = You should take
thou shouldst keep = You should keep
thou wilt = You want

PARABLES OF THE WHEAT AND THE TARES

(Matthew 13, 24 - 30)

Jesus (to his disciples and the crowds):

Just as the weeds are gathered and burned with fire, so will it be at the close of the age. The Son of man will send his angels, and they will gather out of his kingdom all causes of sin and all evildoers, and throw them into the furnace of fire.

(Matthew 13, 40 - 42)

PARABLES OF THE WHEAT AND
THE TARES

nother parable he (Jesus) put before them, (his disciples and the crowds) saying:

♦ *The kingdom of heaven may be compared to a man*
who sowed good seed in his field; but while men
were sleeping, his enemy came and sowed weeds among the
wheat, and went away. So when the plants came up and
bore grain, then the weeds appeared also. And the servants
of the householder came and said to him:

- Sir, did you not sow good seed in your field? How then
has it weeds?

He said to them:

- An enemy has done this.

The servants said to him:

- Then do you want us to go and gather them?

But he said:

- No; lest in gathering the weeds you root up the wheat
along with them. Let both grow together until the harvest; and at harvest time I will tell the reapers, Gather

*the weeds first and bind them in bundles to be burned,
but gather the wheat into my barn.*

(Matthew 13, 24 - 30)

JESUS EXPLAINS THE PARABLES OF
THE WHEAT AND THE TARES

hen he (Jesus) left the crowds and went into the house. And his disciples approached him, saying:

♦ *Explain to us the parable of the weeds of the field.*

He answered:

♦ *The one who sows the good seed is the Son of Man; the field is the world, and the good seed are the children of the kingdom; the weeds are the children of the evil one, and the enemy who sowed them is the devil; the harvest is the end of the age, and the reapers are angels. Just as the weeds are collected and burned up with fire, so will it be at the end of the age. The Son of Man will send his angels, and they will collect out of his kingdom all causes of sin and all evildoers, and they will throw them into the furnace of fire, where there will be weeping and gnashing of teeth. Then the righteous will shine like the sun in the kingdom of their Father. He who has ears, let him hear.*

(Matthew 13, 36 - 43)

THE BIRTH OF JESUS FORETOLD
THE LIFE OF JESUS ILLUSTRATIONS

In the sixth month the angel Gabriel was sent from God to a city of Galilee named Nazareth, to a virgin betrothed to a man whose name was Joseph, of the house of David; and the virgin's name was Mary. And he came to her and said, "Hail, O favored one, the Lord is with you!" But she was greatly troubled at the saying, and considered in her mind what sort of greeting this might be. And the angel said to her, "Do not be afraid, Mary, for you have found favor with God. And behold, you will conceive in your womb and bear a son, and you shall call his name Jesus. He will be great, and will be called the Son of the Most High; and the Lord God will give to him the throne of his father David, and he will reign over the house of Jacob forever; and of his kingdom there will be no end."

(Luke 1, 26 - 33)

THE PARABLE OF THE TENANTS

(Matthew 21, 33 - 46; Mark 12, 1 - 12; Luke 20, 9)

Jesus (to the chief priests
and the Pharisees):

Have you never read in the scriptures: `The very stone which the builders rejected has become the head of the corner; this was the Lord's doing, and it is marvelous in our eyes'? Therefore I tell you, the kingdom of God will be taken away from you and given to a nation producing the fruits of it.

(Matthew 21, 42. 43; Mark 12, 10. 11; Luke 20, 17)

THE PARABLE OF THE TENANTS

Jesus (to the chief priests and the Pharisees):

ear another parable. There was a householder who planted a vineyard, and set a hedge around it, and dug a wine press in it, and built a tower, and let it out to tenants, and went into another country. When the season of fruit drew near, he sent his servants to the tenants, to get his fruit; and the tenants took his servants and beat one, killed another, and stoned another. Again he sent other servants, more than the first; and they did the same to them. Afterward he sent his son to them, saying, `They will respect my son.' But when the tenants saw the son, they said to themselves, `This is the heir; come, let us kill him and have his inheritance.' And they took him and cast him out of the vineyard, and killed him. When therefore the owner of the vineyard comes, what will he do to those tenants?

They said to him:

♦ *He will put those wretches to a miserable death, and let out the vineyard to other tenants who will give him the fruits in their seasons.*

Jesus said to them:

♦ *Have you never read in the scriptures: `The very stone which the builders rejected has become the head of the cor-*

ner; this was the Lord's doing, and it is marvelous in our eyes'? Therefore I tell you, the kingdom of God will be taken away from you and given to a nation producing the fruits of it.

When the chief priests and the Pharisees heard his parables, they perceived that he was speaking about them. But when they tried to arrest him, they feared the multitudes, because they held him to be a prophet.

(Matthew 21, 33 - 46; Mark 12, 1 - 12; Luke 20, 9)

THE PARABLE OF THE SOWER

(Matthew 13, 1 – 9; Mark 4, 1 – 9; Luke 8, 4 – 8)

Jesus (to his disciples and the crowds):

The sower sows the word. And these are the ones along the path, where the word is sown; when they hear, Satan immediately comes and takes away the word which is sown in them. And these in like manner are the ones sown upon rocky ground, who, when they hear the word, immediately receive it with joy; and they have no root in themselves, but endure for a while; then, when tribulation or persecution arises on account of the word, immediately they fall away. And others are the ones sown among thorns; they are those who hear the word, but the cares of the world, and the delight in riches, and the desire for other things, enter in and choke the word, and it proves unfruitful. But those that were sown upon the good soil are the ones who hear the word and accept it and bear fruit, thirtyfold and sixtyfold and a hundredfold.

(Mark 4, 14 - 20; Matthew 13, 19 - 23;
Luke 8, 12 - 15)

THE PARABLE OF THE SOWER

hat same day Jesus went out of the house and sat beside the sea. And great crowds gathered about him, so that he got into a boat and sat there; and the whole crowd stood on the beach. And he told them many things in parables, saying:

♦ *A sower went out to sow. And as he sowed, some seeds fell along the path, and the birds came and devoured them. Other seeds fell on rocky ground, where they had not much soil, and immediately they sprang up, since they had no depth of soil, but when the sun rose they were scorched; and since they had no root they withered away. Other seeds fell upon thorns, and the thorns grew up and choked them. Other seeds fell on good soil and brought forth grain, some a hundredfold, some sixty, some thirty. He who has ears, let him hear.*

(Matthew 13, 1 – 9; Mark 4, 1 – 9; Luke 8, 4 – 8)

JESUS EXPLAINS THE PARABLE
OF THE SOWER

nd when he was alone, those who were about him with the twelve asked him concerning the parables. And he said to them:

♦ *To you has been given the secret of the kingdom of God, but for those outside everything is in parables; so that they may indeed see but not perceive, and may indeed hear but not understand; lest they should turn again, and be forgiven.*

And he said to them:

♦ *Do you not understand this parable? How then will you understand all the parables? The sower sows the word. And these are the ones along the path, where the word is sown; when they hear, Satan immediately comes and takes away the word which is sown in them. And these in like manner are the ones sown upon rocky ground, who, when they hear the word, immediately receive it with joy; and they have no root in themselves, but endure for a while; then, when tribulation or persecution arises on account of the word, immediately they fall away. And others are the ones sown among thorns; they are those who hear the word, but the cares of the world, and the delight in riches, and the desire for other things, enter in and choke the word, and it proves unfruitful. But those that were sown upon the good soil are the ones who hear the word and accept it and bear fruit, thirtyfold and sixtyfold and a hundredfold.*

(Mark 4, 10 – 20; Matthew 13, 10 – 23; Luke 8, 9 – 15)

THE BIRTH OF JESUS
THE LIFE OF JESUS ILLUSTRATIONS

In those days a decree went out from Caesar Augustus that all the world should be enrolled. This was the first enrollment, when Quirinius was governor of Syria. And all went to be enrolled, each to his own city. And Joseph also went up from Galilee, from the city of Nazareth, to Judea, to the city of David, which is called Bethlehem, because he was of the house and lineage of David, to be enrolled with Mary, his betrothed, who was with child. And while they were there, the time came for her to be delivered. And she gave birth to her first-born son and wrapped him in swaddling cloths, and laid him in a manger, because there was no place for them in the inn. And in that region there were shepherds out in the field, keeping watch over their flock by night. And an angel of the Lord appeared to them, and the glory of the Lord shone around them, and they were filled with fear. And the angel said to them, "Be not afraid; for behold, I bring you good news of a great joy which will come to all the people; for to you is born this day in the city of David a Savior, who is Christ the Lord."

(Luke 2, 1 - 11)

THE PARABLE OF THE RICH MAN AND LAZARUS

(Luke 16, 19 - 31)

The rich man (to Abraham):

Then I beg you, father, to send him (Lazarus) to
my father's house, for I have five brothers, so that
he may warn them, lest they also come into this
place of torment.

Abraham:

If they do not hear Moses and the prophets,
neither will they be convinced if some one should
rise from the dead.

(Luke 16, 27. 31)

THE PARABLE OF THE RICH MAN
AND LAZARUS

Jesus (to his disciples and the Jews):

here was a rich man, who was clothed in purple and fine linen and who feasted sumptuously every day. And at his gate lay a poor man named Lazarus, full of sores, who desired to be fed with what fell from the rich man's table; moreover the dogs came and licked his sores. The poor man died and was carried by the angels to Abraham's bosom. The rich man also died and was buried; and in Hades, being in torment, he lifted up his eyes, and saw Abraham far off and Lazarus in his bosom. And he called out:

- Father Abraham, have mercy upon me, and send Lazarus to dip the end of his finger in water and cool my tongue; for I am in anguish in this flame.'

But Abraham said:

- Son, remember that you in your lifetime received your good things, and Lazarus in like manner evil things; but now he is comforted here, and you are in anguish. And besides all this, between us and you a great chasm has been fixed, in order that those who would pass from there to us.

And he said:

- Then I beg you, father, to send him to my father's house for I have five brothers, so that he may warn them, lest they also come into this place of torment.'

But Abraham said:

- They have Moses and the prophets; let them hear them.

And he said:

- No, father Abraham; but if some one goes to them from the dead, they will repent.

He said to him:

- If they do not hear Moses and the prophets, neither will they be convinced if some one should rise from the dead.

(Luke 16, 19 - 31)

THE PARABLE OF THE LOST SON

(Luke 15, 11 - 32)

Father (to his elder son):

Son, you are always with me, and all that is mine is yours. It was fitting to make merry and be glad, for this your brother was dead, and is alive; he was lost, and is found.

(Luke 15, 31. 32)

THE PARABLE OF THE LOST SON

Jesus (to the Pharisees and the scribes):

here was a man who had two sons; and the younger of them said to his father:

- Father, give me the share of property that falls to me.

And he divided his living between them. Not many days later, the younger son gathered all he had and took his journey into a far country, and there he squandered his property in loose living. And when he had spent everything, a great famine arose in that country, and he began to be in want. So he went and joined himself to one of the citizens of that country, who sent him into his fields to feed swine. And he would gladly have fed on the pods that the swine ate; and no one gave him anything. But when he came to himself he said:

- How many of my father's hired servants have bread enough and to spare, but I perish here with hunger! I will arise and go to my father, and I will say to him:Father, I have sinned against heaven and before you; I am no longer worthy to be called your son; treat me as one of your hired servants.

And he arose and came to his father. But while he was yet at a distance, his father saw him and had compassion, and ran and embraced him and kissed him. And the son said to him:

> *- Father, I have sinned against heaven and before you; I am no longer worthy to be called your son.*

But the father said to his servants:

> *- Bring quickly the best robe, and put it on him; and put a ring on his hand, and shoes on his feet; and bring the fatted calf and kill it, and let us eat and make merry; for this my son was dead, and is alive again; he was lost, and is found.*

And they began to make merry. Now his elder son was in the field; and as he came and drew near to the house, he heard music and dancing. And he called one of the servants and asked what this meant. And he said to him:

> *- Your brother has come, and your father has killed the fatted calf, because he has received him safe and sound.'*

But he was angry and refused to go in. His father came out and entreated him, but he answered his father:

> *- Lo, these many years I have served you, and I never disobeyed your command; yet you never gave me a kid, that I might make merry with my friends. But when this son of yours came, who has devoured your living with harlots, you killed for him the fatted calf!*

And he said to him:

- Son, you are always with me, and all that is mine is yours. It was fitting to make merry and be glad, for this your brother was dead, and is alive; he was lost, and is found.

(Luke 15, 11 - 32)

THE BAPTISM OF JESUS
THE LIFE OF JESUS ILLUSTRATIONS

Then Jesus came from Galilee to the Jordan to John, to be baptized by him. John would have prevented him, saying, "I need to be baptized by you, and do you come to me?" But Jesus answered him, "Let it be so now; for thus it is fitting for us to fulfill all righteousness." Then he consented. And when Jesus was baptized, he went up immediately from the water, and behold, the heavens were opened and he saw the Spirit of God descending like a dove, and alighting on him; and lo, a voice from heaven, saying, "This is my beloved Son, with whom I am well pleased."

(Matthew 3, 13 - 17)

THE PARABLE OF THE WEDDING FEAST

(Matthew 22, 1 - 14;   Luke 14, 16 - 24)

Jesus (to the chief priests and the Pharisees):

The kingdom of heaven may be compared to a king who gave a marriage feast for his son, and sent his servants to call those who were invited to the marriage feast; but they would not come. Then he said to his servants:

`The wedding is ready, but those invited were not worthy. Go therefore to the thoroughfares, and invite to the marriage feast as many as you find.'

But when the king came in to look at the guests, he saw there a man who had no wedding garment; and he said to him:

`Friend, how did you get in here without a wedding garment?'

And he was speechless. Then the king said to the attendants:

`Bind him hand and foot, and cast him into the outer darkness; there men will weep and gnash their teeth.'

For many are called, but few are chosen.

(Matthew 22, 2 - 14;   Luke 14, 16 - 24)

THE PARABLE OF THE WEDDING FEAST

Jesus (to the chief priests and the Pharisees):

he kingdom of heaven may be compared to a king who gave a marriage feast for his son, and sent his servants to call those who were invited to the marriage feast; but they would not come. Again he sent other servants, saying:

- Tell those who are invited, Behold, I have made ready my dinner, my oxen and my fat calves are killed, and everything is ready; come to the marriage feast.

But they made light of it and went off, one to his farm, another to his business, while the rest seized his servants, treated them shamefully, and killed them. The king was angry, and he sent his troops and destroyed those murderers and burned their city. Then he said to his servants:

- The wedding is ready, but those invited were not worthy. Go therefore to the thoroughfares, and invite to the marriage feast as many as you find.

And those servants went out into the streets and gathered all whom they found, both bad and good; so the wedding hall was filled with guests.

But when the king came in to look at the guests, he saw there a man who had no wedding garment; and he said to him:

- Friend, how did you get in here without a wedding garment?

And he was speechless. Then the king said to the attendants:

- Bind him hand and foot, and cast him into the outer darkness; there men will weep and gnash their teeth. For many are called, but few are chosen.

(Matthew 22, 2 - 14; Luke 14, 16 - 24)

THE PARABLE OF THE GROWING SEED

(Mark 4, 26 - 29)

Jesus (to his disciples and the crowds):

The kingdom of God is as if a man should scatter seed upon the ground. But when the grain is ripe, at once he puts in the sickle, because the harvest has come.

(Mark 4, 26 . 29)

THE PARABLE OF THE GROWING SEED

Jesus (to his disciples and the crowds):

he kingdom of God is as if a man should scatter seed upon the ground, and should sleep and rise night and day, and the seed should sprout and grow, he knows not how. The earth produces of itself, first the blade, then the ear, then the full grain in the ear. But when the grain is ripe, at once he puts in the sickle, because the harvest has come.

(Mark 4, 26 - 29)

PREACHING AT THE LAKE OF
GENNESARET
THE LIFE OF JESUS ILLUSTRATIONS

And when it was day he departed and went into a lonely place. And the people sought him and came to him, and would have kept him from leaving them; but he said to them, "I must preach the good news of the kingdom of God to the other cities also; for I was sent for this purpose." And he was preaching in the synagogues of Judea.

While the people pressed upon him to hear the word of God, he was standing by the lake of Gennesaret. And he saw two boats by the lake; but the fishermen had gone out of them and were washing their nets. Getting into one of the boats, which was Simon's, he asked him to put out a little from the land. And he sat down and taught the people from the boat.

(Luke 4, 42 - 44; 5, 1 - 3)

34

The parable of the good Samaritan

(Luke 10, 25 - 37)

Jesus (to the lawyer):

Which of these three, do you think, proved neighbor to the man who fell among the robbers?

He said:

The one who showed mercy on him.

And Jesus said to him:

Go and do likewise.

(Luke 10, 36. 37)

THE PARABLE OF THE GOOD SAMARITAN

nd behold, a lawyer stood up to put him to the test, saying:

♦ *Teacher, what shall I do to inherit eternal life?*

He said to him:

♦ *What is written in the law? How do you read?*

And he answered:

♦ *You shall love the Lord your God with all your heart, and with all your soul, and with all your strength, and with all your mind; and your neighbor as yourself.*

And he said to him:

♦ *You have answered right; do this, and you will live.*

But he, desiring to justify himself, said to Jesus:

♦ *And who is my neighbor?*

Jesus replied:

♦ *A man was going down from Jerusalem to Jericho, and he fell among robbers, who stripped him and beat him, and departed, leaving him half dead. Now by chance a priest was going down that road; and when he saw him he passed by on the other side. So likewise a Levite, when he came to the place and saw him, passed by on the other side. But a Samaritan, as he journeyed, came to where he was; and when he saw him, he had compassion, and went to him and bound up his wounds, pouring on oil and wine; then he set him on his own beast and brought him to an inn, and took care of him. And the next day he took out two denarii and gave them to the innkeeper, saying:*

    - Take care of him; and whatever more you spend, I will repay you when I come back.

Which of these three, do you think, proved neighbor to the man who fell among the robbers?

He said:

♦ *The one who showed mercy on him.*

And Jesus said to him:

♦ *Go and do likewise.*

(Luke 10, 25 - 37)

THE PARABLE OF THE LOST SHEEP

(Luke 15, 1 – 7;   Matthew 18, 12. 13)

Jesus (to the Pharisees and the scribes):

I tell you, there will be more joy in heaven over one sinner who repents than over ninetynine righteous persons who need no repentance.

(Luke 15, 7;   Matthew 18, 13)

THE PARABLE OF THE LOST SHEEP

ow the tax collectors and sinners were all drawing near to hear him. And the Pharisees and the scribes murmured, saying:

♦ *This man receives sinners and eats with them.*

So he told them this parable:

♦ *What man of you, having a hundred sheep, if he has lost one of them, does not leave the ninety-nine in the wilderness, and go after the one which is lost, until he finds it? And when he has found it, he lays it on his shoulders, rejoicing. And when he comes home, he calls together his friends and his neighbors, saying to them:*

   - Rejoice with me, for I have found my sheep which was lost.

Just so, I tell you, there will be more joy in heaven over one sinner who repents than over ninety-nine righteous persons who need no repentance.

(Luke 15, 1 – 7;   Matthew 18, 12. 13)

41

JESUS IN SYNAGOGUE

THE LIFE OF JESUS ILLUSTRATIONS

And he came to Nazareth, where he had been brought up; and he went to the synagogue, as his custom was, on the Sabbath day. And he stood up to read; and there was given to him the book of the prophet Isaiah. He opened the book and found the place where it was written, "The Spirit of the Lord is upon me, because he has anointed me to preach good news to the poor. He has sent me to proclaim release to the captives and recovering of sight to the blind, to set at liberty those who are oppressed, to proclaim the acceptable year of the Lord." And he closed the book, and gave it back to the attendant, and sat down; and the eyes of all in the synagogue were fixed on him. And he began to say to them, "Today this scripture has been fulfilled in your hearing." And all spoke well of him, and wondered at the gracious words which proceeded out of his mouth; and they said, "Is not this Joseph's son?"

(Luke 4, 16 - 22)

42

THE PARABLE OF THE LABORERS IN THE VINEYARD

(Matthew 20, 1 - 16)

Jesus (to his disciples
and the crowds):

So the last will be first, and the first last.

(Matthew 20, 16)

THE PARABLE OF THE LABORERS
IN THE VINEYARD

Jesus (to his disciples and the crowds):

or the kingdom of heaven is like a householder who went out early in the morning to hire laborers for his vineyard. After agreeing with the laborers for a denarius a day, he sent them into his vineyard. And going out about the third hour he saw others standing idle in the market place; and to them he said:

-You go into the vineyard too, and whatever is right I will give you.

So they went. Going out again about the sixth hour and the ninth hour, he did the same. And about the eleventh hour he went out and found others standing; and he said to them:

- Why do you stand here idle all day?

They said to him:

- Because no one has hired us.

He said to them:

- You go into the vineyard too.

And when evening came, the owner of the vineyard said to

his steward:

> *- Call the laborers and pay them their wages, beginning with the last, up to the first.*

And when those hired about the eleventh hour came, each of them received a denarius. Now when the first came, they thought they would receive more; but each of them also received a denarius. And on receiving it they grumbled at the house-holder, saying:

> *- These last worked only one hour, and you have made them equal to us who have borne the burden of the day and the scorching heat.*

But he replied to one of them:

> *- Friend, I am doing you no wrong; did you not agree with me for a denarius? Take what belongs to you, and go; I choose to give to this last as I give to you. Am I not alow-ed to do what I choose with what belongs to me? Or do you begrudge my generosity?*

So the last will be first, and the first last.

(Matthew 20, 1 - 16)

THE PARABLE OF THE WIDOW AND THE JUDGE

(Luke 18, 1 - 8)

Jesus (to his disciples
and the crowds):

*And will not God vindicate his elect, who cry to him
day and night? Will he delay long over them? I tell
you, he will vindicate them speedily. Nevertheless,
when the Son of man comes, will he find faith on
earth?*

(Luke 18, 7. 8)

THE PARABLE OF THE WIDOW
AND THE JUDGE

nd he told them a parable, to the effect that they ought always to pray and not lose heart. He said:

♦ *In a certain city there was a judge who neither fear-ed God nor regarded man; and there was a widow in that city who kept coming to him and saying:*

- Vindicate me against my adversary.

For a while he refused; but afterward he said to himself:

- Though I neither fear God nor regard man, yet because this widow bothers me, I will vindicate her, or she will wear me out by her continual coming.

And the Lord said:

♦ *Hear what the unrighteous judge says. And will not God vin-dicate his elect, who cry to him day and night? Will he delay long over them? I tell you, he will vindicate them speedily. Nevertheless,when the Son of man comes, will he find faith on earth?*

(Luke 18, 1 - 8)

THE SERMON ON THE MOUNT
THE LIFE OF JESUS ILLUSTRATIONS

Seeing the crowds, he went up on the mountain, and when he sat down his disciples came to him. And he opened his mouth and taught them, saying: "Blessed are the poor in spirit, for theirs is the kingdom of heaven. "Blessed are those who mourn, for they shall be comforted. "Blessed are the meek, for they shall inherit the earth. "Blessed are those who hunger and thirst for righteousness, for they shall be satisfied. "Blessed are the merciful, for they shall obtain mercy. "Blessed are the pure in heart, for they shall see God. "Blessed are the peacemakers, for they shall be called sons of God. "Blessed are those who are persecuted for righteousness' sake, for theirs is the kingdom of heaven. "Blessed are you when men revile you and persecute you and utter all kinds of evil against you falsely on my account. Rejoice and be glad, for your reward is great in heaven, for so men persecuted the prophets who were before you.

(Matthew 5, 1 - 12)

50

THE PARABLE OF THE TALENTS

(Matthew 25, 13 - 30)

Jesus (to his disciples):

For to every one who has will more be given, and he will have abundance; but from him who has not, even what he has will be taken away.

(Matthew 25, 29)

THE PARABLE OF THE TALENTS

Jesus (to his disciples):

atch therefore, for you know neither the day nor the hour. For it will be as when a man going on a journey called his servants and entrusted to them his property, to one he gave five talents, to another two, to another one, to each according to his ability. Then he went away. He who had received the five talents went at once and traded with them; and he made five talents more. So also, he who had the two talents made two talents more. But he who had received the one talent went and dug in the ground and hid his master's money. Now after a long time the master of those servants came and settled accounts with them. And he who had received the five talents came forward, bringing five talents more, saying:

- *Master, you delivered to me five talents; here I have made five talents more.*

His master said to him:

- *Well done, good and faithful servant; you have been faith ful over a little, I will set you over much; enter into the joy of your master.*

And he also who had the two talents came forward, saying:

- *Master, you delivered to me two talents; here I have made two talents more.*

His master said to him:

> *- Well done, good and faithful servant; you have been faithful over a little, I will set you over much; enter into the joy of your master.*

He also who had received the one talent came forward, saying:

> *- Master, I knew you to be a hard man, reaping where you did not sow, and gathering where you did not winnow; so I was afraid, and I went and hid your talent in the ground. Here you have what is yours.*

But his master answered him:

> *- You wicked and slothful servant! You knew that I reap where I have not sowed, and gather where I have not winnowed? Then you ought to have invested my money with the bankers, and at my coming I should have received what was my own with interest. So take the talent from him, and give it to him who has the ten talents. For to every one who has will more be given, and he will have abundance; but from him who has not, even what he has will be taken away.*

> *And cast the worthless servant into the outer darkness; there men will weep and gnash their teeth.'*

(Matthew 25, 13 – 30)

THE PARABLE OF THE PEARL

(Matthew 13, 45. 46)

Jesus (to his disciples and
the crowds):

*The kingdom of heaven is like a merchant in search
of fine pearls, who, on finding one pearl of great
value, went and sold all that he had and bought it.*

(Mattew 13, 45. 46)

THE PARABLE OF THE PEARL

Jesus (to his disciples and the crowds):

gain, the kingdom of heaven is like a merchant in search of fine pearls, who, on finding one pearl of great value, went and sold all that he had and bought it.

(Matthew 13, 45. 46)

SIGNS OF THE END OF THE AGE
THE LIFE OF JESUS ILLUSTRATIONS

For as the lightning comes from the east and shines as far as the west, so will be the coming of the Son of man. Wherever the body is, there the eagles will be gathered together. "Immediately after the tribulation of those days the sun will be darkened, and the moon will not give its light, and the stars will fall from heaven, and the powers of the heavens will be shaken; then will appear the sign of the Son of man in heaven, and then all the tribes of the earth will mourn, and they will see the Son of man coming on the clouds of heaven with power and great glory; and he will send out his angels with a loud trumpet call, and they will gather his elect from the four winds, from one end of heaven to the other. But of that day and hour no one knows, not even the angels of heaven, nor the Son, but the Father only."

(Matthew 24, 27 - 31, 36)

THE PARABLE OF THE UNFORGIVING SERVANT

(Matthew 18, 23 - 35)

A king (to his servant):

You wicked servant! I forgave you all that debt because you besought me; and should not you have had mercy on your fellow servant, as I had mercy on you? And in anger his lord delivered him to the jailers, till he should pay all his debt.

Jesus (to his disciples):

So also my heavenly Father will do to every one of you, if you do not forgive your brother from your heart.

(Matthew 18, 32 - 35)

THE PARABLE OF THE UNFORGIVING
SERVANT

herefore the kingdom of heaven may be compared to a king who wished to settle accounts with his servants. When he began the reckoning, one was brought to him who owed him ten thousand talents; and as he could not pay, his lord ordered him to be sold, with his wife and children and all that he had, and payment to be made. So the servant fell on his knees, imploring him:

- Lord, have patience with me, and I will pay you everything.

And out of pity for him the lord of that servant released him and forgave him the debt. But that same servant, as he went out, came upon one of his fellow servants who owed him a hundred denarii; and seizing him by the throat he said:

- Pay what you owe.

So his fellow servant fell down and besought him:

- Have patience with me, and I will pay you.

He refused and went and put him in prison till he should pay the debt. When his fellow servants saw what had taken place, they were greatly distressed, and they went and reported to their lord all that had taken place. Then his lord summoned him and said to him:

- You wicked servant! I forgave you all that debt because you besought me; and should not you have had mercy on your fellow servant, as I had mercy on you?

And in anger his lord delivered him to the jailers, till he should pay all his debt.

So also my heavenly Father will do to every one of you, if you do not forgive your brother from your heart.

(Matthew 18, 21 - 35)

THE PARABLE OF THE HIDDEN TREASURE

(Matthew 13, 44)

Jesus (to his disciples
and the crowds):

*The kingdom of heaven is like treasure hidden in a
field, which a man found and covered up; then in his
joy he goes and sells all that he has and buys that
field.*

(Matthew 13, 44)

THE PARABLE OF THE HIDDEN
TREASURE

Jesus (to his disciples and the crowds):

he kingdom of heaven is like treasure hidden in a field, which a man found and covered up; then in his joy he goes and sells all that he has and buys that field.

(Matthew 13, 44)

65

JESUS BLESSES LITTLE CHILDREN
THE LIFE OF JESUS ILLUSTRATIONS

And they were bringing children to him, that he might touch them; and the disciples rebuked them. But when Jesus saw it he was indignant, and said to them, "Let the children come to me, do not hinder them; for to such belongs the kingdom of God. Truly, I say to you, whoever does not receive the kingdom of God like a child shall not enter it." And he took them in his arms and blessed them, laying his hands upon them.

"Truly, I say to you, unless you turn and become like children, you will never enter the kingdom of heaven. Whoever humbles himself like this child, he is the greatest in the kingdom of heaven. Whoever receives one such child in my name receives me; See that you do not despise one of these little ones; for I tell you that in heaven their angels always behold the face of my Father who is in heaven."

(Mark 10, 13 - 16, Matthew 18, 3 - 5, 10, Luke 18, 15 - 17)

66

THE PARABLE OF THE RICH FOOL

(Luke 12, 16 - 31; Matthew 6, 25 - 33)

Jesus (to his disciples and the crowds):

Therefore I tell you, do not be anxious about your life, what you shall eat, nor about your body, what you shall put on. For life is more than food, and the body more than clothing. Consider the ravens: they neither sow nor reap, they have neither storehouse nor barn, and yet God feeds them. Of how much more value are you than the birds! And which of you by being anxious can add a cubit to his span of life? If then you are not able to do as small a thing as that, why are you anxious about the rest? Consider the lilies, how they grow; they neither toil nor spin; yet I tell you, even Solomon in all his glory was not arrayed like one of these. But if God so clothes the grass which is alive in the field today and tomorow is thrown into the oven, how much more will he clothe you, O men of little faith! And do not seek what you are to eat and what you are to drink, nor be of anxious mind. For all the nations of the world seek these things; and your Father know that you need them. Instead, seek his kingdom, and these things shall be yours as well.

(Luke 12, 22 – 31;   Matthew 6, 25 – 33)

THE PARABLE OF THE RICH FOOL

And he told them a parable, saying:

he land of a rich man brought forth plentylly;and he thought to himself:

    - What shall I do, for I have nowhere to store my crops?

And he said:

    - I will do this: I will pull down my barns, and build larger ones; and there I will store all my grain and my goods. And I will say to my soul, Soul, you have ample goods laid up for many years; take your ease, eat, drink, be merry.

But God said to him:

    - Fool! This night your soul is required of you; and the things you have prepared, whose will they be?

So is he who lays up treasure for himself, and is not rich toward God.

And he said to his disciples:

♦ *Therefore I tell you, do not be anxious about your life, what you shall eat, nor about your body, what you shall put on. For life is more than food, and the body more than clothing. Consider the ravens: they neither sow nor reap, they have nei-*

ther storehouse nor barn, and yet God feeds them. Of how much more value are you than the birds! And which of you by being anxious can add a cubit to his span of life? If then you are not able to do as small a thing as that, why are you anxious about the rest? Consider the lilies, how they grow; they neither toil nor spin; yet I tell you, even Solomon in all his glory was not arrayed like one of these. But if God so clothes the grass which is alive in the field today and tomorow is thrown into the oven, how much more will he clothe you, O men of little faith! And do not seek what you are to eat and what you are to drink, nor be of anxious mind. For all the nations of the world seek these things; and your Father know that you need them. Instead, seek his kingdom, and these things shall be yours as well.

(Luke 12, 16 – 31;   Matthew 6, 25 - 33)

THE PARABLE OF THE MUSTARD SEED

(Matthew 13, 31. 32; Mark 4, 30 – 32; Luke 13, 18 – 19)

Jesus (to his disciples
and the crowds):

The kingdom of heaven is like a grain of mustard seed which a man took and sowed in his field; it is the smallest of all seeds, but when it has grown it is the greatest of shrubs and becomes a tree, so that the birds of the air come and make nests in its branches.

(Matthew 13, 31. 32; Mark 4, 30 - 34;
Luke 13, 18. 19)

THE PARABLE OF THE MUSTARD SEED

Jesus (to his disciples and the crowds):

ith what can we compare the kingdom of God, or what parable shall we use for it? It is like a grain of mustard seed, which, when sown upon the ground, is the smallest of all the seeds on earth; yet when it is sown it grows up and becomes the greatest of all shrubs, and puts forth large branches, so that the birds of the air can make nests in its shade.

(Matthew 13, 31. 32; Mark 4, 30 – 32; Luke 13, 18 – 19)

JESUS AND THE SAMARITAN WOMAN
THE LIFE OF JESUS ILLUSTRATIONS

Jacob's well was there, and so Jesus, wearied as he was with his journey, sat down beside the well. It was about the sixth hour. There came a woman of Samaria to draw water. Jesus said to her, "Give me a drink." For his disciples had gone away into the city to buy food. The Samaritan woman said to him, "How is it that you, a Jew, ask a drink of me, a woman of Samaria?" For Jews have no dealings with Samaritans. Jesus answered her, "If you knew the gift of God, and who it is that is saying to you, `Give me a drink,' you would have asked him, and he would have given you living water."

Jesus said to her, "Every one who drinks of this water will thirst again, but whoever drinks of the water that I shall give him will never thirst; the water that I shall give him will become in him a spring of water welling up to eternal life."

(John 4, 6 - 10, 13. 14)

74

THE PARABLE OF THE PERSISTENT FRIEND

(Luke 11, 1 - 13; Matthew 6, 9 - 13;   7, 7 - 11;
Mark 11, 24; John 15, 7)

Jesus (to his disciples):

Ask, and it will be given you; seek, and you will find; knock, and it will be opened to you. For every one who asks receives, and he who seeks finds, and to him who knocks it will be opened.

If you then, who are evil, know how to give good gifts to your children, how much more will the heavenly Father give the Holy Spirit to those who ask him!

(Luke 11, 9 - 13; Matthew 7, 7 - 11; John 15, 7)

THE PARABLE OF THE PERSISTENT FRIEND

e was praying in a certain place, and when he ceased, one of his disciples said to him:

♦ *Lord, teach us to pray, as John taught his disciples.*

And he said to them:

♦ *When you pray, say:*

> *Father, hallowed be thy name.*
> *Thy kingdom come.*
> *Give us each day our daily bread;*
> *and forgive us our sins,*
> *for we ourselves forgive every one*
> *who is indebted to us;*
> *and lead us not into temptation.*

And he said to them:

Which of you who has a friend will go to him at midnight and say to him:

- Friend, lend me three loaves; for a friend of mine has arrived on a journey, and I have nothing to set before him;

And he will answer from within:

- Do not bother me; the door is now shut, and my children are with me in bed; I cannot get up and give you anything?

I tell you, though he will not get up and give him anything because he is his friend, yet because of his importunity he will rise and give him whatever he needs. And I tell you, Ask, and it will be given you; seek, and you will find; knock, and it will be opened to you. For every one who asks receives, and he who seeks finds, and to him who knocks it will be opened.

What father among you, if his son asks for a fish, will instead of a fish give him a serpent; or if he asks for an egg, will give him a scorpion?

If you then, who are evil, know how to give good gifts to your children, how much more will the heavenly Father give the Holy Spirit to those who ask him!

(Luke 11, 1 – 13; Matthew 6, 9 – 13; 7, 7 – 11; Mark 11, 24; John 15, 7)

THE PARABLE OF THE NET

(Matthew 13, 47 - 50)

Jesus (to his disciples):

Again, the kingdom of heaven is like a net which was thrown into the sea and gathered fish of every kind; when it was full, men drew it ashore and sat down and sorted the good into vessels but threw away the bad. So it will be at the close of the age. The angels will come out and separate the evil from the righteous, and throw them into the furnace of fire; there men will weep and gnash their teeth.

(Matthew 13, 47 - 50)

THE PARABLE OF THE NET

Jesus (to his disciples):

gain, the kingdom of heaven is like a net which was thrown into the sea and gathered fish of every kind; when it was full, men drew it ashore and sat down and sorted the good into vessels but threw away the bad. So it will be at the close of the age. The angels will come out and separate the evil from the righteous, and throw them into the furnace of fire; there men will weep and gnash their teeth.

(Matthew 13, 47 - 50)

JESUS PRAYS IN THE GARDEN
THE LIFE OF JESUS ILLUSTRATIONS

And when they had sung a hymn, they went out to the Mount of Olives. Then Jesus said to them, "You will all fall away because of me this night; for it is written, `I will strike the shepherd, and the sheep of the flock will be scattered.' But after I am raised up, I will go before you to Galilee." And taking with him Peter and the two sons of Zebedee, he began to be sorrowful and troubled. Then he said to them, "My soul is very sorrowful, even to death; remain here, and watch with me." And going a little farther he fell on his face and prayed, "My Father, if it be possible, let this cup pass from me; nevertheless, not as I will, but as thou wilt." And he came to the disciples and found them sleeping; and he said to Peter, "So, could you not watch with me one hour? Watch and pray that you may not enter into temptation; the spirit indeed is willing, but the flesh is weak." Again, for the second time, he went away and prayed, "My Father, if this cannot pass unless I drink it, thy will be done." So, leaving them again, he went away and prayed for the third time, saying the same words.

(Matthew 26, 30 - 32, 37 - 42, 44)

THE PARABLE OF THE TWO SONS

(Matthew 21, 28 - 32)

Jesus (to the chief priests and the
elders of the people):

*Truly, I say to you, the tax collectors and the
harlots go into the kingdom of God before you.
For John came to you in the way of righteousness,
and you did not believe him, but the tax collectors
and the harlots believed him; and even when you
saw it, you did not afterward repent and believe him.*

(Matthew 21, 31. 32)

THE PARABLE OF THE TWO SONS

Jesus (to the chief priests and the elders of the people):

hat do you think? A man had two sons; and he went to the first and said:

- Son, go and work in the vineyard today.

And he answered:

- I will not!

But afterward he repented and went. And he went to the second and said the same; and he answered:

- I go, sir,

but did not go. Which of the two did the will of his father?

They said:

♦ *The first.*

Jesus said to them:

♦ *Truly, I say to you, the tax collectors and the harlots go into the kingdom of God before you. For John came to you in the way of righteousness, and you did not believe him, but the tax collectors and the harlots believed him; and even when you saw it, you did not afterward repent and believe him.*

(Matthew 21, 28 - 32)

THE PARABLE OF THE YEAST

(Luke 13, 20. 21;   Matthew 13, 33 - 35)

Jesus (to his disciples
and the crowds):

*The kingdom of heaven is like leaven which a woman
took and hid in three measures of flour, till it was all
leavened.*

(Matthew 13, 33;   Luke 13, 20. 21)

THE PARABLE OF THE YEAST

Jesus (to his disciples and the crowds):

o what shall I compare the kingdom of God? It is like leaven which a woman took and hid in three measures of flour, till it was all leavened.

(Luke 13, 20. 21, Matthew 13, 33)

All this Jesus said to the crowds in parables; indeed he said nothing to them without a parable. This was to fulfil what was spoken by the prophet:

♦ *I will open my mouth in parables, I will utter what has been hidden since the foundation of the world.*

(Matthew 13, 34. 35)

JESUS PRAYS ON THE MOUNT OF OLIVES
THE LIFE OF JESUS ILLUSTRATIONS

And he came out, and went, as was his custom, to the Mount of Olives; and the disciples followed him. And when he came to the place he said to them, "Pray that you may not enter into temptation." And he withdrew from them about a stone's throw, and knelt down and prayed, "Father, if thou art willing, remove this cup from me; nevertheless not my will, but thine, be done." And when he rose from prayer, he came to the disciples and found them sleeping for sorrow, and he said to them, "Why do you sleep? Rise and pray that you may not enter into temptation."

(Luke 22, 39 - 46)

90

THE PARABLE OF THIS GENERATION

(Matthew 11, 2 - 19; Luke 7, 16 - 35; 16, 16)

Jesus (to John the Baptist):

The blind receive their sight and the lame walk, lepers are cleansed and the deaf hear, and the dead are raised up, and the poor have good news preached to them. And blessed is he who takes no offense at me.

(Matthew 11, 5. 6; Luke 7, 22. 23)

THE PARABLE OF THIS GENERATION

ow when John heard in prison about the deeds of the Christ, he sent word by his disciples and said to him:

♦ *Are you he who is to come, or shall we look for another?*

And Jesus answered them:

♦ *Go and tell John what you hear and see: the blind receive their sight and the lame walk, lepers are cleansed and the deaf hear, and the dead are raised up, and the poor have good news preached to them. And blessed is he who takes no offense at me.*

As they went away, Jesus began to speak to the crowds concerning John:

♦ *What did you go out into the wilderness to behold? A reed shaken by the wind? Why then did you go out? To see a man clothed in soft raiment? Behold, those who wear soft raiment are in kings' houses. Why then did you go out? To see a prophet? Yes, I tell you, and more than a prophet. This is he of whom it is written:*

  - Behold, I send my messenger before thy face, who shall prepare thy way before thee.

Truly, I say to you, among those born of women there has risen no one greater than John the Baptist; yet he who is least in the kingdom of heaven is greater than he. From the days of John the Baptist until now the kingdom of heaven has suffered violence, and men of violence take it by force. For all the prophets and the law prophesied until John; and if you are willing to accept it, he is Elijah who is to come. He who has ears to hear, let him hear. But to what shall I compare this generation? It is like children sitting in the market places and calling to their playmates, `We piped to you, and you did not dance; we wailed, and you did not mourn.' For John came neither eating nor drinking, and they say:

- He has a demon,

the Son of man came eating and drinking, and they say:

- Behold, a glutton and a drunkard, a friend of tax collectors and sinners!

Yet wisdom is justified by her deeds.

(Matthew 11, 2 - 19; Lk 7, 16 - 35; 16, 16)

94

The parable of the two house builders

(Matthew 7, 24 - 29)

Jesus (to his disciples and the crowds):

Every one then who hears these words of mine and does them will be like a wise man who built his house upon the rock; and the rain fell, and the floods came, and the winds blew and beat upon that house, but it did not fall, because it had been founded on the rock.

(Matthew 7, 24 - 29)

THE PARABLE OF THE TWO HOUSE BUILDERS

Jesus (to his disciples and the crowds):

very one then who hears these words of mine and does them will be like a wise man who built his house upon the rock; and the rain fell, and the floods came, and the winds blew and beat upon that house, but it did not fall, because it had been founded on the rock.
And every one who hears these words of mine and does not do them will be like a foolish man who built his house upon the sand; and the rain fell, and the floods came, and the winds blew and beat against that house, and it fell; and great was the fall of it.

And when Jesus finished these sayings, the crowds were astonished at his teaching, for he taught them as one who had authority, and not as their scribes.

(Matthew 7, 24 - 29)

97

JESUS FEEDS THE FOUR THOUSAND
THE LIFE OF JESUS ILLUSTRATIONS

Then Jesus called his disciples to him and said, "I have compassion on the crowd, be-cause they have been with me now three days, and have nothing to eat; and I am unwilling to send them away hungry, lest they faint on the way." And the disciples said to him, "Where are we to get bread enough in the desert to feed so great a crowd?" And Jesus said to them, "How many loaves have you?" They said, "Seven, and a few small fish." And commanding the crowd to sit down on the ground, he took the seven loaves and the fish, and having given thanks he broke them and gave them to the disciples, and the disciples gave them to the crowds. And they all ate and were satisfied; and they took up seven baskets full of the broken pieces left over. Those who ate were four thousand men, besides women and children. And sending away the crowds, he got into the boat and went to the region of Magadan.

(Matthew 15, 32 - 39)

THE PARABLE OF THE SHREWD MANAGER

(Luke 16, 1 - 13)

Jesus (to his disciples):

No servant can serve two masters; for either he will hate the one and love the other, or he will be devoted to the one and despise the other. You cannot serve God and mammon.

(Luke 16, 13)

THE PARABLE OF THE SHREWD MANAGER

Jesus (to his disciples):

here was a rich man who had a steward, and charges were brought to him that this man was wasting his goods. And he called him and said to him:

- What is this that I hear about you? Turn in the account of your stewardship, for you can no longer be steward.

And the steward said to himself:

- What shall I do, since my master is taking the steward-ship away from me? I am not strong enough to dig, and I am ashamed to beg. I have decided what to do, so that people may receive me into their houses when I am put out of the stewardship.

So, summoning his master's debtors one by one, he said to the first:

- How much do you owe my master?

He said:

- A hundred measures of oil.

And he said to him:

- Take your bill, and sit down quickly and write fifty.

Then he said to another:

- And how much do you owe?

He said:

- A hundred measures of wheat.

He said to him:

- Take your bill, and write eighty.

The master commended the dishonest steward for his shrewdness; for the sons of this world are more shrewd in dealing with their own generation than the sons of light. And I tell you, make friends for yourselves by means of unrighteous mammon, so that when it fails they may receive you into the eternal habitations. He who is faithful in a very little is faithful also in much; and he who is dishonest in a very little is dishonest also in much. If then you have not been faithful in the unrighteous mammon, who will entrust to you the true riches?: And if you have not been faithful in that which is another's, who will give you that which is your own? No servant can serve two masters; for either he will hate the one and love the other, or he will be devoted to the one and despise the other. You cannot serve God and mammon.

(Luke 16, 1 - 13)

THE PARABLE OF THE FAITHFUL
OR THE WICKED SLAVE
(Matthew)

(Matthew 24, 42 - 51; Mark 13, 33 - 37; Luke 12,
39. 40. 42 - 46)

Jesus (to his disciples):

Watch therefore, for you do not know on what day your Lord is coming. But know this, that if the householder had known in what part of the night the thief was coming, he would have watched and would not have let his house be broken into. Therefore you also must be ready; for the Son of man is coming at an hour you do not expect.

(Matthew 24, 42 - 44;   Mark 13, 35 - 37;
Luke 12, 39. 40)

THE PARABLE OF THE FAITHFUL OR THE WICKED SLAVE (Matthew)

Jesus (to his disciples):

atch therefore, for you do not know on what day your Lord is coming. But know this, that if the householder had known in what part of the night the thief was coming, he would have watched and would not have let his house be broken into. Therefore you also must be ready; for the Son of man is coming at an hour you do not expect. Who then is the faithful and wise servant, whom his master has set over his household, to give them their food at the proper time? Blessed is that servant whom his master when he comes will find so doing. Truly, I say to you, he will set him over all his possessions. But if that wicked servant says to himself:

- My master is delayed

and begins to beat his fellow servants, and eats and drinks with the drunken, the master of that servant will come on a day when he does not expect him and at an hour he does not know, and will punish him, and put him with the hypocrites; there men will weep and gnash their teeth.

(Matthew 24, 42 – 51; Mark 13, 33 – 37; Luke 12, 42 - 48)

105

JESUS CALMS A STORM
THE LIFE OF JESUS ILLUSTRATIONS

On that day, when evening had come, he said to them, "Let us go across to the other side." And leaving the crowd, they took him with them in the boat, just as he was. And other boats were with him. And a great storm of wind arose, and the waves beat into the boat, so that the boat was already filling. But he was in the stern, asleep on the cushion; and they woke him and said to him, "Teacher, do you not care if we perish?" And he awoke and rebuked the wind, and said to the sea, "Peace! Be still!" And the wind ceased, and there was a great calm. He said to them, "Why are you afraid? Have you no faith?" And they were filled with awe, and said to one another, "Who then is this, that even wind and sea obey him?"

(Mark 4, 35 - 41)

106

THE PARABLE OF THE LOST COIN

(Luke 15, 8 - 10)

Jesus (to the Pharisees
and the scribes):

*Just so, I tell you, there is joy before the angels of God
over one sinner who repents.*

(Luke 15, 10)

THE PARABLE OF THE LOST COIN

Jesus (to the Pharisees and the scribes):

r what woman, having ten silver coins, if she loses one coin, does not light a lamp and sweep the house and seek diligently until she finds it? And when she has found it, she calls together her friends and neighbors, saying:

- Rejoice with me, for I have found the coin which I had lost.

Just so, I tell you, there is joy before the angels of God over one sinner who repents.

(Luke 15, 8 – 10)

JESUS RAISES LAZARUS FROM THE DEAD
THE LIFE OF JESUS ILLUSTRATIONS

Jesus said, "Take away the stone." Martha, the sister of the dead man, said to him, "Lord, by this time there will be an odor, for he has been dead four days." Jesus said to her, "Did I not tell you that if you would believe you would see the glory of God?" So they took away the stone. And Jesus lifted up his eyes and said, "Father, I thank thee that you for having heard me. I knew that you always hear me, but I have said this on account of the people standing by, that they may believe that you send me." When he had said this, he cried with a loud voice, "Lazarus, come out." The dead man came out, his hands and feet bound with bandages, and his face wrapped with a cloth. Jesus said to them, "Unbind him, and let him go." Many of the Jews therefore, who had come with Mary and had seen what he did, believed in him.

(John 11, 39 - 45)

110

The parable of the pharisee and the tax collector

(Luke 18, 9 - 14)

Jesus (to his disciples
and the crowds):

*For every one who exalts himself will be humbled,
but he who humbles himself will be exalted.*

(Luke 18, 14)

THE PARABLE OF THE PHARISEE AND THE TAX COLLECTOR

e also told this parable to some who trusted in themselves that they were righteous and despised others:

♦ *Two men went up into the temple to pray, one a Pharisee and the other a tax collector. The Pharisee stood and prayed thus with himself:*

- *God, I thank thee that I am not like other men, extortioners, unjust, adulterers, or even like this tax collector. I fast twice a week, I give tithes of all that I get.*

But the tax collector, standing far off, would not even lift up his eyes to heaven, but beat his breast, saying:

- *God, be merciful to me a sinner!*

I tell you, this man went down to his house justified rather than the other; for every one who exalts himself will be humbled, but he who humbles himself will be exalted.

(Luke 18, 9 - 14)

113

THE TRANSFIGURATION
THE LIFE OF JESUS ILLUSTRATIONS

And after six days Jesus took with him Peter and James and John his brother, and led them up a high mountain apart. And he was transfigured before them, and his face shone like the sun, and his garments became white as light. And behold, there appeared to them Moses and Elijah, talking with him. And Peter said to Jesus, "Lord, it is well that we are here; if you wish, I will make three booths here, one for you and one for Moses and one for Elijah." He was still speaking, when lo, a bright cloud overshadowed them, and a voice from the cloud said, "This is my beloved Son, with whom I am well pleased; listen to him." When the disciples heard this, they fell on their faces, and were filled with awe.

(Matthew 17, 1 - 6)

114

THE PARABLE OF THE FAITHFUL OR THE WICKED SLAVE

(Luke)

(Luke 12, 42 – 48)

Jesus (to his disciples):

And that servant who knew his master's will, but did not make ready or act according to his will, shall receive a severe beating. But he who did not know, and did what deserved a beating, shall receive a light beating. Every one to whom much is given, of him will much be required; and of him to whom men commit much they will demand the more.

(Luke 12, 47. 48)

THE PARABLE OF THE FAITHFUL OR THE WICKED SLAVE (Luke)

And the Lord said (to his disciples):

ho then is the faithful and wise steward, whom his master will set over his household, to give them their portion of food at the proper time? Blessed is that servant whom his master when he comes will find so doing. Truly, I say to you, he will set him over all his possessions. But if that servant says to himself:

- My master is delayed in coming,

and begins to beat the menservants and the maidservants, and to eat and drink and get drunk, the master of that servant will come on a day when he does not expect him and at an hour he does not know, and will punish him, and put him with the unfaithful. And that servant who knew his master's will, but did not make ready or act according to his will, shall receive a severe beating. But he who did not know, and did what deserved a beating, shall receive a light beating. Every one to whom much is given, of him will much be required; and of him to whom men commit much they will demand the more.

(Luke 12, 42 - 48)

117

THE TRIUMPHANT ENTRY INTO JERUSALEM
THE ILLUSTRATIONS FROM THE LIFE OF JESUS

And when they drew near to Jerusalem and came to Bethphage, to the Mount of Olives, then Jesus sent two disciples, saying to them, "Go into the village opposite you, and immediately you will find an ass tied, and a colt with her; untie them and bring them to me. The disciples went and did as Jesus had directed them; they brought the ass and the colt, and put their garments on them, and he sat thereon. Most of the crowd spread their garments on the road, and others cut branches from the trees and spread them on the road. And the crowds that went before him and that followed him shouted, "Hosanna to the Son of David! Blessed is he who comes in the name of the Lord! Hosanna in the highest!" And when he entered Jerusalem, all the city was stirred, saying, "Who is this?" And the crowds said, "This is the prophet Jesus from Nazareth of Galilee."

(Matthew 21, 1. 2. 6 - 11)

THE PARABLE OF THE UNFRUIT-FUL FIG TREE

(Luke 13, 6 - 9)

A householder (to his vinedresser):

Lo, these three years I have come seeking fruit on thisfig tree, and I find none. Cut it down; why should it use up the ground?

And he answered him:

Let it alone, sir, this year also, till I dig about it and put on manure. And if it bears fruit next year, well and good; but if not, you can cut it down.

(Luke 13, 7 - 9)

THE PARABLE OF THE UNFRUITFUL FIG TREE

Jesus (to his disciples and the crowds):

man had a fig tree planted in his vineyard; and he came seeking fruit on it and found none. And he said to the vinedresser:

- Lo, these three years I have come seeking fruit on this fig tree, and I find none. Cut it down; why should it use up the ground?

And he answered him:

- Let it alone, sir, this year also, till I dig about it and put on manure. And if it bears fruit next year, well and good; but if not, you can cut it down.

(Luke 13, 6 - 9)

121

THE LAST SUPPER

THE LIFE OF JESUS ILLUSTRATIONS

When it was evening, he sat at table with the twelve disciples; and as they were eating, he said, "Truly, I say to you, one of you will betray me." And they were very sorrowful, and began to say to him one after another, "Is it I, Lord?" He answered, "He who has dipped his hand in the dish with me, will betray me. The Son of man goes as it is written of him, but woe to that man by whom the Son of man is betrayed! It would have been better for that man if he had not been born." Judas, who betrayed him, said, "Is it I, Master?" He said to him, "You have said so." Now as they were eating, Jesus took bread, and blessed, and broke it, and gave it to the disciples and said, "Take, eat; this is my body." And he took a cup, and when he had given thanks he gave it to them, saying, "Drink of it, all of you; for this is my blood of the covenant, which is poured out for many for the forgiveness of sins. I tell you I shall not drink again of this fruit of the vine until that day when I drink it new with you in my Father's kingdom."

(Matthew 26, 20 - 29)

THE PARABLE OF THE TEN BRIDESMAIDS

(Matthew 25, 1 – 13)

Jesus (to his disciples):

Watch therefore, for you know neither the day nor the hour (in which the Son of Man is coming).

(Matthew 25, 13)

THE PARABLE OF THE TEN BRIDESMAIDS

Jesus (to his disciples):

hen the kingdom of heaven shall be compared to ten maidens who took their lamps and went to meet the bridegroom. Five of them were foolish, and five were wise. For when the foolish took their lamps, they took no oil with them; but the wise took flasks of oil with their lamps. As the bridegroom was delayed, they all slumbered and slept. But at midnight there was a cry, `Behold, the bridegroom! Come out to meet him.' Then all those maidens rose and trimmed their lamps. And the foolish said to the wise, `Give us some of your oil, for our lamps are going out.' But the wise replied, `Perhaps there will not be enough for us and for you; go rather to the dealers and buy for yourselves.' And while they went to buy, the bridegroom came, and those who were ready went in with him to the marriage feast; and the door was shut. Afterward the other maidens came also, saying:

- Lord, lord, open to us.

But he replied:

- Truly, I say to you, I do not know you.

Watch therefore, for you know neither the day nor the hour (in which the Son of Man is coming).

(Matthew 25, 1 – 13)

THE ASCENSION
THE LIFE OF JESUS ILLUSTRATIONS

Luke: 'In the first book, O Theophilus, I have dealt with all that Jesus began to do and teach, until the day when he was taken up, after he had given commandment through the Holy Spirit to the apostles whom he had chosen. To them he presented himself alive after his passion by many proofs, appearing to them during forty days, and speaking of the kingdom of God. And while staying with them he charged them not to depart from Jerusalem, but to wait for the promise of the Father, which, he said, "you heard from me, for John baptized with water, but before many days you shall be baptized with the Holy Spirit." So when they had come together, they asked him, "Lord, will you at this time restore the kingdom to Israel?" He said to them, "It is not for you to know times or seasons which the Father has fixed by his own authority. But you shall receive power when the Holy Spirit has come upon you; and you shall be my witnesses in Jerusalem and in all Judea and Samaria and to the end of the earth. "And when he had said this, as they were looking on, he was lifted up, and a cloud took him out of their sight.'

(Acts 1, 1 - 9)

126

THE PARABLE OF THE GOOD SHEPHERD

(John 10, 1 - 18)

Jesus (to the Jews):

I am the good shepherd. The good shepherd lays down his life for the sheep. For this rea-son the Father loves me, because I lay down my life, that I may take it again. No one takes it from me, but I lay it down of my own accord. I have power to lay it down, and I have power to take it again; this charge I have received from my Father.

(John 10, 11. 17. 18)

THE PARABLE OF THE GOOD SHEPHERD

Jesus (to the Jews):

ruly, truly, I say to you, he who does not enter the sheepfold by the door but climbs in by another way, that man is a thief and a robber; but he who enters by the door is the shepherd of the sheep. To him the gatekeeper opens; the sheep hear his voice, and he calls his own sheep by name and leads them out. When he has brought out all his own, he goes before them, and the sheep follow him, for they know his voice. A stranger they will not follow, but they will flee from him, for they do not know the voice of strangers.

This figure Jesus used with them, but they did not understand what he was saying to them. So Jesus again said to them:

♦ *Truly, truly, I say to you, I am the door of the sheep. All who came before me are thieves and robbers; but the sheep did not heed them. I am the door; if any one enters by me, he will be saved, and will go in and out and find pasture. The thief comes only to steal and kill and destroy; I came that they may have life, and have it abundantly. I am the goodshepherd. The good shepherd lays down his life for the sheep. He who is a hireling and not a shepherd, whose own the sheep are not, sees the wolf coming and leaves the sheep and flees; and the wolf snatches them and scatters them. He flees because not, sees the wolf coming and leaves the sheep and flees; and the wolf snatches them and scatters them. He flees because he is a hireling and cares nothing for the sheep. I am the good shepherd; I know my own and my own know me, as the Father knows me and I know the Father; and I lay down my life for the sheep. And I have other sheep, that are not of this fold; I must bring them also, and they will heed my voice. So there shall be one flock, one shepherd. For this reason the Father loves me, because I lay down my life, that I may take it again. No one takes it from me, but I lay it down of my own accord. I have power to lay it down, and I have power to take it again; this charge I have received from my Father.*

(John 10, 1 - 18)

CONTENTS

THE PARABLES OF JESUS

1. Parables of the Wheat and Tares   1

   Jesus Explains the Parable   5

2. The Parable of the Tenants   7

3. The Parable of the Sower   11

   Jesus Explains the Parable   14

4. The Parable of the Rich Man and Lazarus   17

5. The Parable of the Lost Son   21

6. The Parable of the Wedding Feast   27

7. The Parable of the Growing Seed   31

8. The Parable of the Good Samaritan   35

9. The Parable of the Lost Sheep   39

10. The Parable of the Laborers in the Vineyard   43

11. The Parable of the Widow and the Judge   47

12. The Parable of the Talents   51

13. The Parable of the Pearl   55

14. The Parable of the Unforgiving Servant   59

15. The Parable of the Hidden Treasure   63

16. The Parable of the Rich Fool   67

17. The Parable of the Mustard Seed   71

18. The Parable of the Persistent Friend   75

19. The Parable of the Net   79

20. The Parable of the Two Sons   83

21. The Parable of the Yeast   87

22. The Parable of This Generation   91

23. The Parable of the Two House Builders   95

24. The Parable of the Shrewd Manager   99

25. The Parable of the Faithful or the Wicked
    Slave (Matthew)   103

26. The Parable of the Lost Coin   107

27. The Parable of the Pharisee and the Tax
    Collector   111

28. The Parable of the Faithful or the Wicked
    Slave (Luke)   115

29. The Parable of the Unfruitful Fig Tree   119

30. The Parable of the Ten Bridesmaids   123

31. The Parable of the Good Shepherd   127

THE ILLUSTRATIONS FROM THE LIFE
OF JESUS

1. The Birth of Jesus Foretold   6

2. The Birth of Jesus   16

3. The Baptism of Jesus   26

4. Preaching at the Lake of Gennesaret   34

5. Jesus in Synagogue   42

6. The Sermon on the Mount   50

7. Signs of the End of the Age   58

8. Jesus Blesses Little Children   66

9. Jesus and the Samaritan Woman   74

10. Jesus Prays in the Garden   82

11. Jesus Prays on the Mount of Olives   90

12. Jesus Feeds the Four Thousand   98

13. Jesus Calms a Storm   106

14. Jesus Raises Lazarus from the Dead   110

15. The Transfiguration   114

16. The Triumphant Entry into Jerusalem   118

17. The Last Supper   122

18. The Ascension   126